**Date: 6/24/19**

**BR 975.3 CHA
Chang, Kirsten,
The Washington Monument /**

SYMBOLS OF AMERICAN FREEDOM

# The Washington Monument

by Kirsten Chang

BLASTOFF! READERS

BELLWETHER MEDIA • MINNEAPOLIS, MN

Note to Librarians, Teachers, and Parents:

**Blastoff! Readers** are carefully developed by literacy experts and combine standards-based content with developmentally appropriate text.

**Level 1** provides the most support through repetition of high-frequency words, light text, predictable sentence patterns, and strong visual support.

**Level 2** offers early readers a bit more challenge through varied simple sentences, increased text load, and less repetition of high-frequency words.

**Level 3** advances early-fluent readers toward fluency through increased text and concept load, less reliance on visuals, longer sentences, and more literary language.

**Level 4** builds reading stamina by providing more text per page, increased use of punctuation, greater variation in sentence patterns, and increasingly challenging vocabulary.

**Level 5** encourages children to move from "learning to read" to "reading to learn" by providing even more text, varied writing styles, and less familiar topics.

Whichever book is right for your reader, Blastoff! Readers are the perfect books to build confidence and encourage a love of reading that will last a lifetime!

This edition first published in 2019 by Bellwether Media, Inc.

No part of this publication may be reproduced in whole or in part without written permission of the publisher. For information regarding permission, write to Bellwether Media, Inc., Attention: Permissions Department, 6012 Blue Circle Drive, Minnetonka, MN 55343.

Library of Congress Cataloging-in-Publication Data

Names: Chang, Kirsten, 1991- author.
Title: The Washington Monument / by Kirsten Chang.
Description: Minneapolis, MN : Bellwether Media, Inc., 2019. |
    Series: Blastoff! Readers: Symbols of American Freedom | Includes bibliographical references and index.
Identifiers: LCCN 2018030383 (print) | LCCN 2018031099 (ebook) | ISBN 9781681036496 (ebook) |
    ISBN 9781626179189 (hardcover : alk. paper) | ISBN 9781618914958 (pbk. : alk. paper)
Subjects: LCSH: Washington Monument (Washington, D.C.)–Juvenile literature. | Washington, George,
    1732-1799–Monuments–Washington (D.C.)–Juvenile literature. | Washington (D.C.)–Buildings, structures,
    etc.–Juvenile literature.
Classification: LCC F203.4.W3 (ebook) | LCC F203.4.W3 C47 2019 (print) | DDC 975.3–dc23
LC record available at https://lccn.loc.gov/2018030383

Editor: Rebecca Sabelko      Designer: Andrea Schneider

Printed in the United States of America, North Mankato, MN.

# Table of Contents

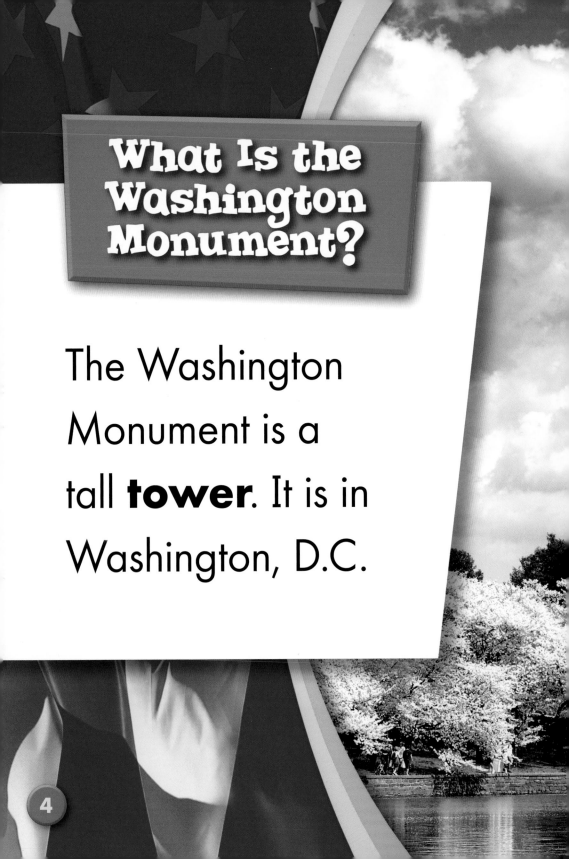

# What Is the Washington Monument?

The Washington Monument is a tall **tower**. It is in Washington, D.C.

It honors George Washington. He fought for American **freedom**.

George
Washington
statue

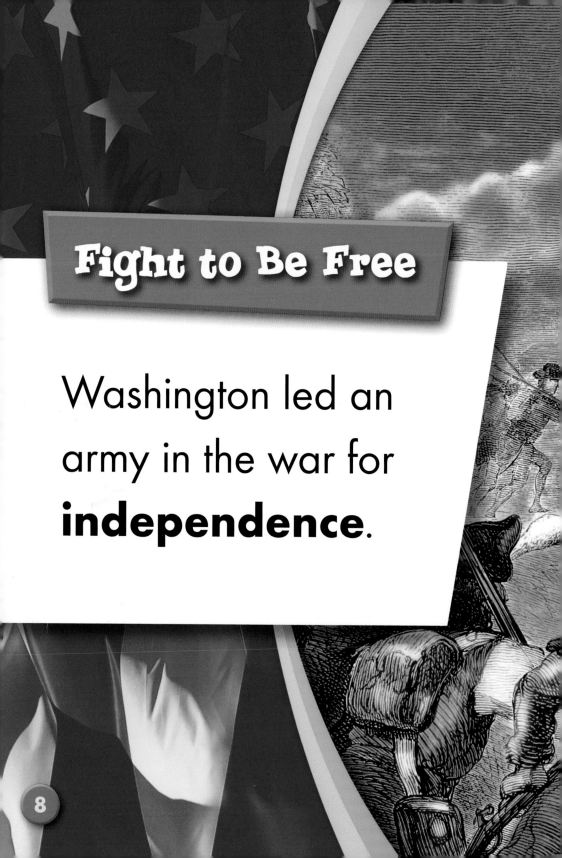

# Fight to Be Free

Washington led an army in the war for **independence**.

George Washington

He helped write the **Constitution**. It stated rules for the country.

the signing of
the Constitution

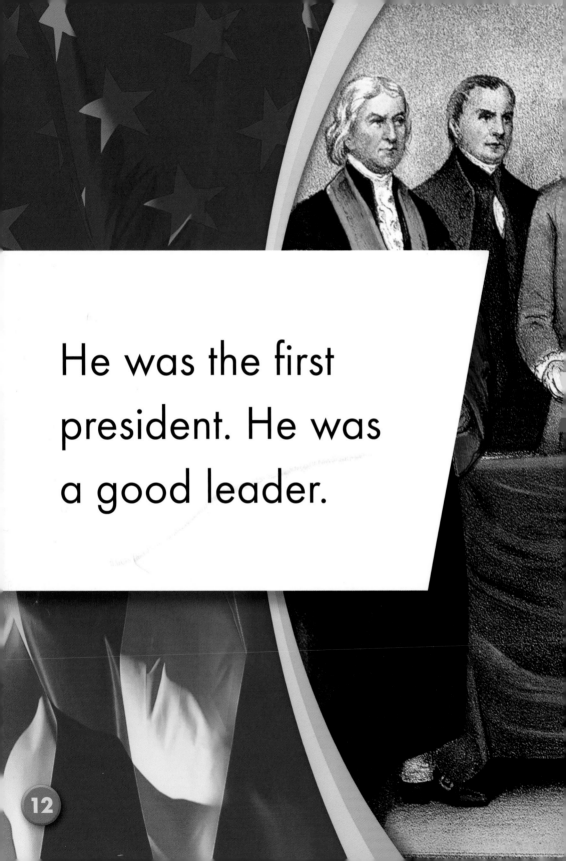

He was the first president. He was a good leader.

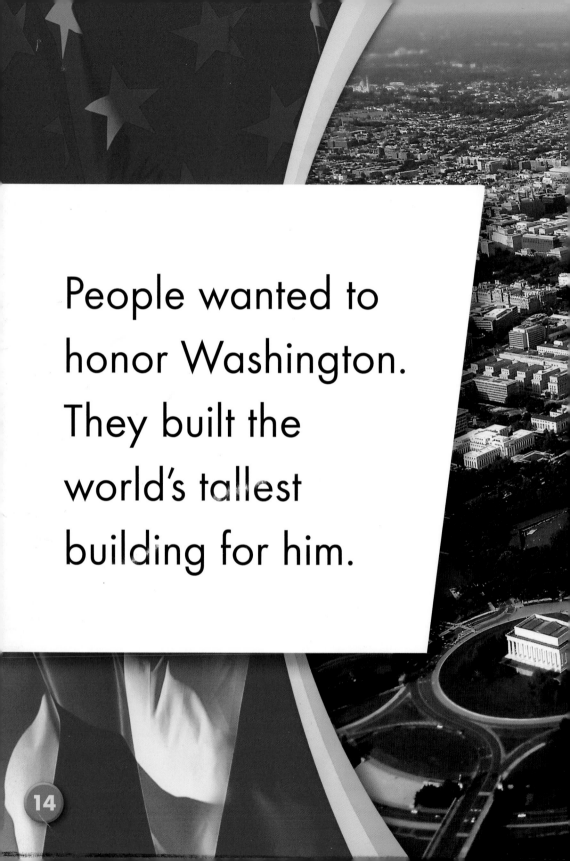

People wanted to honor Washington. They built the world's tallest building for him.

# World's Tallest Building

**1884**
Washington
Monument
**555 feet
(169 meters)
tall**

**2018**
Burj Khalifa
**2,717 feet
(828 meters)
tall**

# A Great Man

Americans visit to learn about the nation's history.

They look up
at the tower
with wonder.

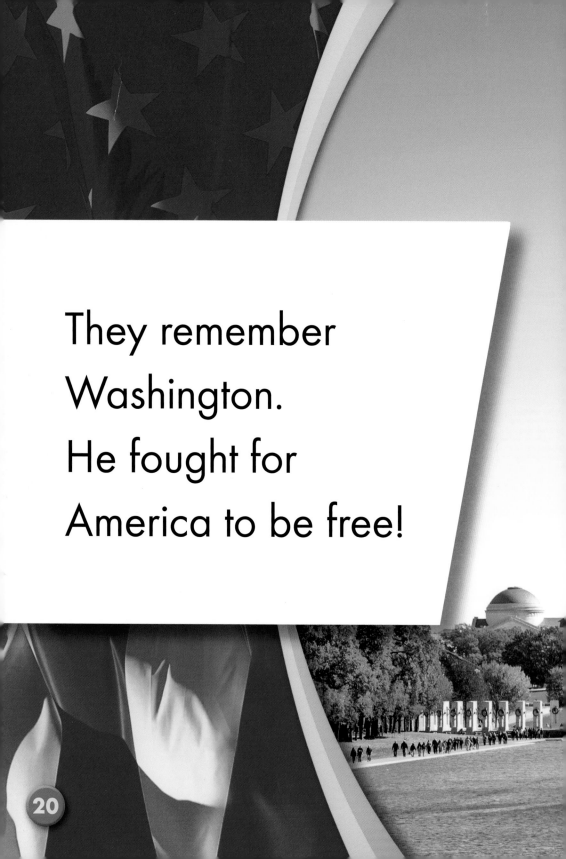

They remember Washington. He fought for America to be free!

# Glossary

**Constitution**

the highest law of the U.S. government

**independence**

the state of being free from the power of others

**freedom**

the state of being free

**tower**

a tall building

# To Learn More

## AT THE LIBRARY

Carr, Aaron. *Washington Monument*.
New York, N.Y.: AV2 by Weigl, 2014.

Marcovitz, Hal. *Washington Monument:
Memorial to a Founding Father*. Philadelphia,
Pa.: Mason Crest, 2015.

Rawson, Katherine. *Washington Monument*.
Minneapolis, Minn.: Bullfrog Books, 2018.

## ON THE WEB

# FACTSURFER

Factsurfer.com gives you
a safe, fun way to find
more information.

1. Go to www.factsurfer.com.

2. Enter "Washington Monument" into the
   search box.

3. Click the "Surf" button and select your
   book cover to see a list of related web sites.

# Index

The images in this book are reproduced through the courtesy of: CTD Photography, front cover, p. 3; Carol M. Highsmith's America, Library of Congress/ Wiki Commons, pp. 4-5; RomanSlavik.com, pp. 6-7; Prisma Archivo/ Alamy, pp. 8-9; The Indian Reporter/ Wiki Commons, pp. 10-11; Glasshouse Images/ Alamy, pp. 12-13; vPaulTech LLC, pp. 14-15; 4kclips, pp. 16-17; Worawat Dechatiwong, pp. 18-19; AlbertPego, pp. 20-21; Sean Locke Photography, p. 22 (upper left); fstop123, p. 22 (bottom left); Monkey Business Images, p. 22 (upper right); meunierd, p. 22 (bottom right).